Confidence Code

Confidence Code

Matthew Petchinsky

CONTENTS

Confidence Code: Building Unshakable Self-Belief
By: Matthew Petchinsky

Introduction: The Myth of Natural Confidence and the Art of Cultivating Inner Confidence

Confidence is one of the most sought-after qualities in human existence. It's a trait that, when fully embraced, empowers individuals to navigate life with a sense of assurance, clarity, and purpose. Yet, despite its universal appeal, confidence often feels elusive, as though it is a natural gift bestowed upon a select few while others are left to struggle with self-doubt. This perception, however, is a myth—a misconception that keeps many from understanding that confidence is not an inherent trait but a skill that can be cultivated from within.

The Myth of Natural Confidence

From a young age, society teaches us to admire confident people—those who speak eloquently, take bold actions, and seem at ease in any situation. We're told, often indirectly, that confidence is a natural characteristic, a fixed trait that some people are simply born with. This creates the illusion that if you don't naturally exude self-assurance, you are somehow destined to live a life of insecurity.

This myth is reinforced by media portrayals of confident individuals. Characters in movies, TV shows, and social media influencers seem effortlessly self-assured, reinforcing the idea that confidence is as innate as the color of one's eyes. What these portrayals fail to show is the unseen effort, struggles, and personal development that often underpin genuine confidence. Believing in the myth of natural confidence can lead to a paralyzing cycle of self-comparison, self-doubt, and, ultimately, inaction.

The truth is that confidence is not about being fearless or perfect. It's not an inherent quality that some are born with and others are not. Confidence is a skill—a practice of self-belief and resilience that anyone can develop. By understanding this, you unlock the first step toward cultivating lasting confidence from within.

How to Create Confidence from Within

Creating confidence from within begins with dismantling the myths and shifting your focus inward. At its core, confidence is about trust—trust in your abilities, your decisions, and your value as a person. This trust isn't dependent on external validation or perfect outcomes but on your willingness to embrace imperfection and growth.

Here's a roadmap to building inner confidence:

1. **Self-Awareness and Acceptance**

   Confidence starts with knowing who you are. This means acknowledging your strengths and talents while also accepting your flaws and limitations. Self-awareness isn't about fixing everything; it's about understanding yourself deeply and authentically. When you accept yourself as a whole, you build the foundation for confidence that doesn't waver in the face of setbacks.

2. **Embracing Vulnerability**

   Contrary to popular belief, confidence is not about masking fears or vulnerabilities. True confidence comes from embracing these aspects of yourself and recognizing that they make you human, relatable, and resilient. When you stop fearing vulnerability, you open yourself to growth and connection.

3. **Reframing Failure**

   Failure is often seen as the opposite of confidence, but in reality, it is one of its greatest teachers. Each setback provides an opportunity to learn, adapt, and strengthen your resolve. Confidence grows when you view failure not as a reflection of your worth but as a stepping stone toward success.

4. **Taking Consistent Action**

   Confidence is built through action. It's not enough to think positively or affirm your worth; you must take steps, however small, toward your goals. Each action reinforces your belief in your abilities and creates a positive feedback loop. Over time, these small victories accumulate into a profound sense of self-assurance.

5. **Cultivating a Growth Mindset**

   Confidence thrives in a growth-oriented environment. When you view challenges as opportunities to learn and believe that your abilities can be developed with effort, you build resilience and adaptability—key components of confidence.

6. **Practicing Self-Compassion**

   The journey to confidence is not linear. There will be moments of doubt and struggle, but self-compassion ensures that you remain kind to yourself during these times. Treat yourself with the same understanding and encouragement you would offer a close friend, and you'll find it easier to move forward.

7. **Connecting to Your Purpose**

   Confidence is deeply tied to a sense of purpose. When you align your actions with your values and goals, you tap into a source of intrinsic motivation that fuels self-belief. Purpose gives your confidence direction and sustains it through adversity.

A Path Toward Empowerment

The journey to creating confidence from within is not a quick fix; it's a lifelong practice. It requires patience, dedication, and a willingness to confront your fears and limitations. But the rewards are immeasurable. When you cultivate inner confidence, you free yourself from the need for external validation, allowing you to live authentically and unapologetically.

In the chapters ahead, we will explore practical tools, insights, and strategies to help you build unshakable confidence from the inside out. Together, we'll break free from the myth of natural confidence and unlock your full potential. Remember, confidence isn't about being perfect—it's about being empowered to face life's challenges with courage and self-belief. The power to create this confidence lies within you, waiting to be discovered and nurtured. Let's begin.

Chapter 1: The Confidence Blueprint

Confidence is often mistaken as a fleeting feeling or a superficial trait, but at its core, it is a deeply rooted state of being. It's a mindset that empowers you to face challenges, make decisions, and live authentically. To cultivate confidence, we must first understand how it works and identify the unique roadblocks that stand in the way of your personal growth. This chapter will serve as the blueprint for your confidence journey, laying the foundation for transformative and lasting change.

Understanding How Confidence Works

Confidence is not a static attribute; it is dynamic and evolves with your experiences, mindset, and actions. At its essence, confidence is composed of three interconnected elements:

1. **Self-Belief**

   Self-belief is the cornerstone of confidence. It is the internal conviction that you are capable of handling whatever life throws your way. This belief doesn't mean you will always succeed; it means you trust yourself to learn, adapt, and persevere regardless of the outcome.

2. **Competence**

   Confidence often grows from competence—the mastery of skills and knowledge. The more you practice and improve in a given area, the more confident you become in your ability to succeed. This competence breeds trust in your abilities and minimizes fear of failure.

3. **Resilience**

   Resilience is your ability to recover from setbacks and maintain self-assurance in the face of adversity. Confidence is not about never falling; it's about knowing you can get back up, learn from the experience, and move forward stronger than before.

These three pillars of confidence work in tandem, reinforcing one another to create a solid foundation. The process is iterative: as you take action, learn, and grow, your confidence increases, which in turn empowers you to take on greater challenges.

Identifying Your Personal Roadblocks

While the blueprint for confidence applies universally, the obstacles that hinder it are deeply personal. Identifying and addressing your unique roadblocks is a crucial step in your journey toward building lasting self-assurance.

1. **Fear of Failure**

   The fear of failure is one of the most common barriers to confidence. It manifests as a fear of rejection, embarrassment, or loss, and often leads to procrastination or avoidance. This fear is rooted in the belief that failure defines your worth, which couldn't be further from the truth.
   - **Reflection Exercise:** Write down a recent failure and list what you learned from it. Consider how this lesson can be a stepping stone for future success.

2. **Negative Self-Talk**

   The inner critic can be a powerful adversary to confidence. Negative self-talk undermines your self-belief by magnifying your flaws, downplaying your strengths, and instilling doubt.
   - **Awareness Practice:** Start noticing the negative phrases you tell yourself. Replace them with empowering statements, such as, "I am capable of growth" or "I deserve to try."

3. **Comparison with Others**

   Comparing yourself to others erodes confidence by making you feel inadequate or "less than." Social media and societal expectations often amplify this tendency, creating an unrealistic standard for success.
   - **Reframe Your Perspective:** Remind yourself that everyone's journey is unique, and comparison is like measuring

apples against oranges. Focus on your own progress instead.

4. **Lack of Preparation**

A lack of preparation can lead to self-doubt. Whether it's an unpracticed skill or unfamiliar situation, entering unprepared can make you feel uncertain and insecure.

- ° **Action Plan:** Identify areas where preparation can boost your confidence. This might mean practicing a skill, researching a topic, or rehearsing a presentation.

5. **Past Trauma or Conditioning**

Negative experiences from your past, such as criticism, rejection, or failure, can create emotional blocks to confidence. These experiences may lead to limiting beliefs like "I'm not good enough" or "I'll never succeed."

- ° **Healing Strategy:** Consider journaling or seeking professional support to address unresolved issues. Recognizing and challenging these beliefs is essential for breaking free from their grip.

6. **Perfectionism**

Perfectionism is the unrealistic expectation of flawlessness. It often results in fear of taking action, as any perceived imperfection feels like a failure.

- ° **Challenge Perfectionism:** Aim for progress, not perfection. Embrace the idea that mistakes are opportunities for learning and growth.

Your Confidence Blueprint in Action

To create a confidence blueprint tailored to your needs, start by addressing the following questions:

1. **What are my current strengths, and how can I build upon them?**

   Confidence often starts with recognizing what you're already good at. Celebrate your achievements and identify ways to further develop your strengths.

2. **What are my biggest roadblocks to confidence?**

   Use the list above to identify the barriers that resonate most with you. Write them down and consider how they've impacted your self-assurance in the past.

3. **What actions can I take today to overcome these roadblocks?**

   Create a list of small, actionable steps to tackle each obstacle. For example, if fear of failure is holding you back, commit to trying something new, even if the outcome is uncertain.

4. **What does confidence look and feel like for me?**

   Visualize your confident self. What are you doing? How are you feeling? What beliefs and actions align with this vision? This mental image will serve as a guiding star for your journey.

Laying the Foundation for Lasting Confidence

Your confidence blueprint is a living document—a roadmap that evolves as you grow. By understanding how confidence works and confronting your personal roadblocks, you empower yourself to take intentional steps toward self-assurance. Remember, confidence is not about never feeling fear or doubt; it's about trusting yourself to take action despite them.

Chapter 2: Small Wins, Big Gains

Building confidence is not about making a single, monumental leap forward. Instead, it's a process of steady, incremental progress. This chapter focuses on the concept of achieving "small wins" and why they matter profoundly in the journey to lasting confidence. By understanding and applying the principle of small victories, you will lay a foundation for continuous growth and build momentum toward greater self-assurance.

Building Confidence Incrementally

Imagine trying to climb a mountain without taking the first step. The summit may seem daunting, even unattainable, when viewed from the base. But with each small step, the peak comes closer into view. Confidence works the same way—it is built step by step, one small win at a time.

Incremental progress is effective because it:

1. **Reduces Overwhelm**

   Tackling a massive goal or overcoming a significant fear all at once can feel intimidating. Breaking it down into smaller, manageable tasks makes the process more approachable and reduces the likelihood of giving up.

2. **Builds Positive Momentum**

   Each small win creates a ripple effect. The sense of accomplishment you feel from achieving a minor goal energizes you to take on the next challenge, creating a cycle of confidence-building success.

3. **Fosters Consistency**

   Confidence is not a one-time achievement; it's a skill that requires ongoing practice. Small, consistent actions help you build habits that reinforce self-assurance over time.

4. **Increases Resilience**

   Small wins allow you to experiment, learn, and grow without the high stakes of larger goals. They provide opportunities to bounce back from minor setbacks and strengthen your resilience.

Why Small Victories Matter

Small victories are the building blocks of confidence. While they may seem insignificant in isolation, their cumulative effect can be transformative. Here's why they matter:

1. **Psychological Boost**

   Each small win triggers the brain's reward system, releasing dopamine—a chemical associated with feelings of pleasure and motivation. This positive reinforcement encourages you to keep pushing forward.

2. **Reinforces Self-Efficacy**

   Self-efficacy is your belief in your ability to achieve specific outcomes. Small wins provide evidence that you are capable, reinforcing this belief and strengthening your overall confidence.

3. **Shifts Your Identity**

   As you accumulate small wins, you begin to see yourself differently. For example, if you consistently make small progress toward healthier habits, you'll start to identify as someone who is disciplined and capable of change.

4. **Encourages Action**

   Success breeds success. When you experience the satisfaction of a small victory, you're more likely to take action again, creating a virtuous cycle of growth and achievement.

5. **Creates a Domino Effect**

   Small wins often lead to larger ones. Overcoming one minor challenge can set off a chain reaction, opening the door to greater opportunities and accomplishments.

How to Build Confidence Through Small Wins

To harness the power of small wins, follow these strategies:

1. **Set Micro-Goals**

   Break down larger goals into smaller, achievable tasks. For instance, instead of aiming to "become more confident at public speaking," start with practicing a short speech in front of a mirror or a trusted friend.

   - **Example:** If your goal is to exercise regularly, begin with a 5-minute workout each day. As you build the habit, gradually increase the time and intensity.

2. **Celebrate Every Achievement**

   Recognize and celebrate your small victories, no matter how minor they may seem. Celebrations don't have to be elaborate; a simple acknowledgment of your progress can reinforce your efforts.

   - **Tip:** Keep a journal of your accomplishments, noting how each one makes you feel and what it contributes to your overall growth.

3. **Start Where You Are**

   Confidence is built by taking action, even if you start small. Don't wait for the perfect circumstances or skill level. Begin with what you have and grow from there.

   - **Example:** If you're shy about networking, start by attending virtual events where you can engage without the pressure of face-to-face interaction.

4. **Focus on Progress, Not Perfection**

   Confidence comes from recognizing and valuing improvement, not from achieving flawlessness. Celebrate the fact that you're moving forward, even if the steps are small and imperfect.

   - **Mindset Shift:** Replace "I haven't done enough" with "I'm proud of the progress I've made."

5. **Leverage Past Wins**

Reflect on past achievements, no matter how small. Use these moments as proof that you are capable of success.

- ◦ **Reflection Exercise:** Write down three past successes and how they made you feel. Remind yourself of these wins when self-doubt arises.

6. **Create a System of Accountability**

Share your goals with someone you trust or join a community that supports your growth. Knowing that others are rooting for you can motivate you to stay consistent.

- ◦ **Example:** Join a group of like-minded individuals who share similar goals, such as a writing circle, fitness class, or professional development group.

Examples of Small Wins That Build Confidence

Here are practical examples of small wins in various areas of life:

- **Professional Confidence**:
  - ◦ Sending an email to a potential mentor.
  - ◦ Completing a small project ahead of schedule.
  - ◦ Speaking up in a meeting, even if it's just to agree with someone else's point.
- **Social Confidence**:
  - ◦ Introducing yourself to a new colleague.
  - ◦ Smiling and making eye contact with a stranger.
  - ◦ Starting a conversation with someone you don't know well.
- **Personal Confidence**:
  - ◦ Trying a new recipe and succeeding.
  - ◦ Learning a simple skill, such as changing a lightbulb or fixing a minor tech issue.
  - ◦ Setting a boundary and sticking to it.
- **Physical Confidence**:

- ◦ Completing a short workout or walk.
- ◦ Trying a new fitness class or activity.
- ◦ Drinking one extra glass of water each day.

The Compound Effect of Small Wins

The power of small wins lies in their ability to compound over time. Each small victory builds upon the last, creating exponential growth in your confidence and abilities.

Consider the metaphor of planting a seed. At first, it may seem like nothing is happening, but with consistent care and nourishment, the seed grows into a thriving plant. Similarly, small wins may seem inconsequential at first, but their cumulative impact can lead to remarkable transformations.

Your First Steps Toward Big Gains

Now that you understand the importance of small wins, it's time to put this knowledge into action. Start by identifying one area of your life where you'd like to build confidence. Then, outline a series of micro-goals and commit to taking the first step today.

Remember, every small victory is a step closer to the confident, empowered version of yourself. By focusing on progress rather than perfection and celebrating each win along the way, you'll unlock a wellspring of confidence that will propel you toward bigger and bolder achievements.

Chapter 3: Conquering Self-Doubt

Self-doubt is one of the most persistent obstacles to confidence. It whispers that you're not good enough, not capable enough, or not deserving of success. This inner critic can feel overwhelming, undermining your self-assurance and holding you back from reaching your full potential. In this chapter, we will explore effective techniques to silence your inner critic and rewire the negative self-talk that feeds self-doubt.

By understanding the roots of self-doubt and implementing strategies to counteract it, you'll gain the tools to transform your inner dialogue into a source of encouragement and empowerment.

Understanding the Inner Critic

The inner critic is an internal voice that often stems from past experiences, societal conditioning, or fear of failure. While it may sometimes appear to protect you from risks, its approach is often harsh and counterproductive, focusing on your perceived flaws rather than your strengths.

Self-doubt can manifest in various ways:

- Fear of failure or rejection.
- Reluctance to try new things.
- Overthinking or second-guessing decisions.
- Belief that success is due to luck rather than ability (imposter syndrome).

Recognizing when your inner critic is speaking is the first step toward conquering self-doubt.

Techniques to Silence Your Inner Critic

Silencing your inner critic doesn't mean suppressing it entirely. Instead, it's about understanding, challenging, and reframing the negative messages it conveys. Here are proven techniques to take control:

1. **Identify the Voice**

   Pay attention to the moments when your inner critic speaks. Write down its messages to make them tangible and easier to analyze.

   - **Exercise:** Keep a journal for one week, noting any negative thoughts you have about yourself. Include the context in which they occur and the emotions they evoke.

2. **Name Your Inner Critic**

   Giving your inner critic a name can help you distance yourself from its negativity. For example, you might call it "Doubtful Debbie" or "Critical Carl." When you name it, you can recognize its voice as separate from your true self.

   - **Action Step:** When the critic speaks, say, "That's just [name] talking. I don't have to listen."

3. **Challenge the Critic's Messages**

   Once you've identified your inner critic's statements, question their validity. Often, these messages are exaggerated or outright false.

   - **Ask Yourself:**
     - What evidence supports this thought?
     - What evidence contradicts it?
     - Is this thought based on facts or assumptions?
     - Would I say this to a friend in the same situation?

4. **Reframe the Criticism**

   Transform negative statements into constructive feedback. For example, "I'll never be good at this" can become, "I need more practice to improve." This reframing shifts your focus from limitations to opportunities for growth.

- ◦ **Exercise:** Rewrite three negative thoughts as positive, actionable statements.

5. **Use Mindfulness to Create Distance**

Mindfulness helps you observe your thoughts without judgment. Instead of reacting to your inner critic, you can acknowledge its presence and choose not to engage.

- ◦ **Practice:** When a negative thought arises, take a deep breath and say, "I notice this thought, but it doesn't define me."

6. **Replace Criticism with Compassion**

Treat yourself with the same kindness and understanding you would offer a close friend. Self-compassion can counteract the harshness of your inner critic and create a supportive inner environment.

- ◦ **Mantra:** "I am doing my best, and that is enough."

7. **Visualize Success**

Replace self-doubt with positive imagery. Visualizing yourself succeeding can counteract the critic's negative predictions and build your confidence.

- ◦ **Exercise:** Spend 5 minutes daily visualizing a specific goal you want to achieve. Picture yourself taking steps toward it and feeling proud of your progress.

8. **Set Boundaries with Your Inner Critic**

Decide when and how much attention to give your inner critic. You don't have to entertain every negative thought.

- ◦ **Technique:** Imagine a mental "stop sign" when the critic becomes overwhelming, signaling yourself to redirect your focus.

Rewiring Negative Self-Talk

Negative self-talk is a habit, and like any habit, it can be rewired with consistent effort. Here's how to transform your inner dialogue:

1. **Identify Core Beliefs**

   Negative self-talk often stems from deep-seated beliefs about yourself. For example, "I'll never succeed" may reflect a belief that you're not capable. Identifying these beliefs is the first step to changing them.
   - **Exercise:** Write down your recurring negative thoughts and trace them back to the underlying beliefs.

2. **Create Affirmations**

   Affirmations are positive statements that counteract negative self-talk. They remind you of your strengths and potential.
   - **Example:** Replace "I'm not good enough" with "I am capable and worthy of success."
   - **Tip:** Repeat affirmations daily, especially in moments of doubt.

3. **Focus on Strengths**

   Shift your attention from your perceived weaknesses to your strengths. Recognizing what you're good at builds self-belief and counters negativity.
   - **Exercise:** List five strengths or accomplishments each day.

4. **Adopt a Growth Mindset**

   A growth mindset emphasizes learning and improvement over fixed abilities. Instead of saying, "I can't do this," say, "I can't do this yet, but I can learn."
   - **Mantra:** "Every challenge is an opportunity to grow."

5. **Surround Yourself with Positivity**

   The people and environments you engage with influence your self-talk. Surround yourself with supportive individuals who uplift you and limit exposure to negativity.

- ◦ **Action Step:** Seek out mentors, friends, or groups that inspire confidence and encouragement.

6. **Practice Gratitude**

   Gratitude shifts your focus from what's lacking to what's present and positive in your life. This practice fosters optimism and reduces the power of negative self-talk.
   - ◦ **Gratitude Journal:** Each day, write down three things you're grateful for.

Building a Supportive Inner Voice

The ultimate goal of conquering self-doubt is to cultivate an inner voice that supports and empowers you. Here are ways to nurture this voice:

- **Be Your Own Cheerleader:** Celebrate your achievements, no matter how small. Remind yourself of your progress and potential.
- **Practice Self-Forgiveness:** Let go of mistakes and view them as learning opportunities.
- **Embrace Imperfection:** Recognize that no one is perfect, and striving for progress is more important than achieving perfection.

Your Confidence Breakthrough

Conquering self-doubt requires patience, persistence, and a willingness to challenge deeply ingrained thought patterns. By silencing your inner critic and rewiring negative self-talk, you'll unlock a wellspring of confidence that allows you to take bold actions, embrace growth, and live authentically.

Chapter 4: Confidence in Action

Confidence, when cultivated, is more than just an internal state—it becomes a transformative force in your external world. It affects how you approach relationships, pursue goals, and navigate high-stakes situations. This chapter will guide you in applying the confidence you've built to practical aspects of life, helping you thrive in relationships and achieve your ambitions. We will also delve into strategies to maintain and project confidence when faced with high-pressure or high-stakes situations.

Applying Confidence to Relationships

Confidence is a cornerstone of healthy, meaningful relationships. It empowers you to communicate effectively, establish boundaries, and foster deeper connections with others. Whether in friendships, family dynamics, or romantic partnerships, confidence enhances how you relate to the people around you.

1. **Communicating with Confidence**

   Communication is at the heart of all relationships. Confidence enables you to express your thoughts, feelings, and needs clearly and respectfully.

   - **Active Listening:** Confidence isn't just about speaking; it's also about listening. Pay attention to the other person's words, tone, and body language.
   - **Assertiveness:** Be direct and honest about your needs and desires without being aggressive. For example, instead of saying, "You never listen to me," say, "I feel unheard when my ideas aren't acknowledged."
   - **Non-Verbal Communication:** Project confidence through your body language—maintain eye contact, stand tall, and use open gestures.

2. **Establishing Boundaries**

Confident people know their limits and aren't afraid to set boundaries. Boundaries protect your emotional well-being and show others that you value yourself.

- **How to Set Boundaries:** Use clear, respectful language. For example, "I appreciate your enthusiasm, but I need some quiet time to focus."
- **Enforce Boundaries:** Confidence means standing firm when boundaries are tested. Politely but firmly remind others of your limits if necessary.

3. **Building Trust and Connection**

Confidence fosters trust and connection by encouraging authenticity. When you're confident, you can show up as your true self, which invites others to do the same.

- **Vulnerability:** Confidence includes the courage to be vulnerable. Share your thoughts and feelings openly, even if it feels uncomfortable.
- **Supportiveness:** Confident individuals uplift others. Celebrate their successes and offer encouragement during challenges.

Applying Confidence to Goals

Confidence is a key ingredient in goal-setting and achievement. It motivates you to take action, persevere through setbacks, and celebrate progress along the way.

1. **Setting Ambitious Yet Achievable Goals**

   Confident people aim high, but they also understand the importance of setting realistic, actionable goals.
   - **SMART Goals:** Ensure your goals are Specific, Measurable, Achievable, Relevant, and Time-bound. For example, "I want to write a book in six months" is more actionable than "I want to be a writer."
   - **Break It Down:** Divide larger goals into smaller milestones to make them less overwhelming and more attainable.

2. **Overcoming Fear of Failure**

   Confidence helps you view failure as a stepping stone rather than a dead end.
   - **Reframe Failure:** Instead of thinking, "I failed," say, "This didn't work, but I learned something valuable."
   - **Celebrate Effort:** Recognize and reward yourself for trying, even if the outcome isn't perfect.

3. **Staying Motivated**

   Confidence sustains motivation by reminding you of your abilities and the progress you've made.
   - **Visualize Success:** Regularly imagine achieving your goals and how it will feel.
   - **Track Progress:** Keep a journal or checklist to monitor milestones and celebrate small wins.

Strategies for High-Stakes Situations

High-stakes situations—job interviews, public speaking, or crucial conversations—can challenge even the most confident individuals. The key is to channel your confidence effectively to navigate these moments with grace and composure.

1. **Preparation is Power**

   Confidence thrives on preparation. The more you know and practice, the more secure you'll feel.
   - **Research:** For example, if you're interviewing for a job, study the company, role, and industry trends.
   - **Practice:** Rehearse speeches, presentations, or difficult conversations in advance. Practice with a trusted friend or in front of a mirror.

2. **Master Your Mindset**

   Confidence begins in the mind. Cultivate a mindset that supports your success.
   - **Positive Affirmations:** Repeat empowering statements, such as, "I am capable and prepared."
   - **Visualization:** Before the event, close your eyes and visualize yourself succeeding. Picture the setting, your actions, and the positive outcome.
   - **Focus on the Moment:** Avoid fixating on potential outcomes. Concentrate on what you can control in the present.

3. **Use Confident Body Language**

   Your body communicates your confidence (or lack thereof) before you even speak.
   - **Posture:** Stand or sit upright with your shoulders back.
   - **Eye Contact:** Maintain eye contact to show engagement and self-assurance.

    ◦ **Gestures:** Use open, purposeful hand movements to reinforce your points.

4. **Control Your Breathing**

Nervousness can disrupt your confidence, but controlled breathing can help you stay calm and focused.

    ◦ **Technique:** Practice the 4-7-8 method—inhale for 4 seconds, hold for 7 seconds, and exhale for 8 seconds. Repeat until you feel grounded.

5. **Embrace the Power of Pausing**

In high-stakes situations, silence can be your ally. Pausing before responding shows thoughtfulness and gives you time to collect your thoughts.

    ◦ **Example:** In a job interview, pause briefly before answering a complex question to ensure your response is clear and concise.

6. **Leverage Support Systems**

Even in high-pressure moments, you don't have to go it alone. Confident people know when to seek support.

    ◦ **Mentors and Peers:** Reach out to trusted individuals for advice or encouragement.

    ◦ **Community Resources:** Join groups or forums related to your goal or situation for shared experiences and tips.

7. **Dealing with Setbacks**

Confidence isn't about avoiding failure but handling it with resilience.

    ◦ **Recovery Plan:** If something goes wrong, focus on what you can learn and how to improve.

    ◦ **Stay Positive:** Remind yourself that one setback doesn't define your abilities or future success.

Putting Confidence Into Practice

Applying confidence in relationships, goals, and high-stakes situations requires ongoing effort. Here are practical ways to start:

1. **Daily Confidence Rituals**

   Incorporate habits that reinforce confidence into your daily routine. For example:
   - Start each day with a positive affirmation.
   - Spend 10 minutes visualizing your goals.
   - Practice one act of courage, such as striking up a conversation with a stranger.

2. **Reflect and Adjust**

   After each significant interaction or experience, reflect on what went well and what you can improve. Use these insights to refine your approach.

3. **Celebrate Successes**

   Recognize your achievements, big and small. Celebrating reinforces your confidence and motivates you to keep striving.

Your Confidence in Action

Confidence is not just an abstract quality; it's a tool you can use to transform your life. By applying your confidence to relationships, goals, and high-stakes situations, you'll unlock new opportunities and overcome challenges with greater ease.

As you practice these strategies, you'll find that confidence becomes second nature—a guiding force that empowers you to connect authentically, achieve ambitiously, and rise to any occasion.

Chapter 5: Owning Your Power

Confidence isn't about never facing setbacks; it's about how you respond to them. Life will inevitably present challenges that test your self-belief, but true confidence lies in your ability to maintain your inner power through those moments. In this chapter, we'll explore how to preserve your confidence during setbacks and develop a presence that radiates authentic self-belief, inspiring yourself and others.

Owning your power is not about being invulnerable; it's about embracing your humanity and leveraging your inner strength to navigate life's ups and downs with grace and resilience.

Maintaining Confidence During Setbacks

Setbacks can shake your confidence, but they also offer opportunities for growth and self-discovery. By reframing these moments and employing strategies to stay grounded, you can emerge stronger and more self-assured.

1. **Reframe Setbacks as Lessons**

   Instead of viewing setbacks as failures, see them as opportunities to learn and grow. Every challenge carries a lesson that can enhance your skills, resilience, or perspective.
   - **Exercise:** After experiencing a setback, ask yourself:
     - What went wrong, and why?
     - What can I learn from this experience?
     - How can I use this knowledge to improve in the future?
   - **Example:** If you didn't get the job you wanted, reflect on how you can refine your interview skills or strengthen your qualifications for the next opportunity.

2. **Practice Emotional Regulation**

Setbacks can trigger intense emotions, but maintaining confidence requires staying composed and centered.

- ◦ **Techniques:**
  - ▪ **Deep Breathing:** Use controlled breathing exercises, such as the 4-7-8 method, to calm your nervous system.
  - ▪ **Grounding:** Focus on the present moment by engaging your senses (e.g., notice what you see, hear, and feel around you).
  - ▪ **Self-Talk:** Replace catastrophic thoughts with affirming ones, such as, "This is temporary, and I'll find a way through."

3. **Lean on Your Support System**

Confidence doesn't mean going it alone. Surround yourself with people who uplift and encourage you during tough times.

- ◦ **Action Step:** Share your experiences with a trusted friend, mentor, or therapist who can offer perspective and guidance.

4. **Celebrate Progress, Not Perfection**

Setbacks often arise from aiming too high too fast. Focus on incremental progress rather than perfection.

- ◦ **Tip:** Reflect on how far you've come, even if you haven't yet reached your ultimate goal.

5. **Create a Resilience Ritual**

Develop a go-to routine that helps you reset after a setback.

- ◦ **Example:** This could include journaling, meditating, exercising, or engaging in a creative activity. These practices can help you process emotions and regain your sense of control.

6. **Revisit Your Strengths and Achievements**

During challenging times, remind yourself of your past successes and strengths. This can help you rebuild your confidence and re-focus on what you can control.

- **Exercise:** Write down five achievements you're proud of and the strengths you used to accomplish them. Reflect on how those strengths can help you overcome your current challenge.

How to Radiate Authentic Self-Belief

Confidence is magnetic when it's genuine. Authentic self-belief isn't about pretending to have it all together—it's about embracing who you are, imperfections and all, and showing up with sincerity and purpose.

1. **Embrace Authenticity**

   Confidence begins with accepting and expressing your true self. Authenticity means aligning your actions, words, and values, creating a sense of integrity and self-respect.
   - **Reflection:** Ask yourself:
     - What are my core values, and how do I live them?
     - Are my goals aligned with who I truly am?
   - **Action Step:** Let go of people-pleasing habits that force you to act against your values or interests.

2. **Speak with Clarity and Conviction**

   The way you communicate can convey confidence and authenticity.
   - **Tips for Speaking Confidently:**
     - Use clear and concise language. Avoid filler words like "um" or "I think."
     - Take your time. Pausing before speaking shows thoughtfulness.
     - Match your tone and body language to your message.

3. **Lead with Vulnerability**

   Authentic confidence includes the courage to be vulnerable. Sharing your struggles or uncertainties, when appropriate, can strengthen connections and build trust.
   - **Example:** In a team meeting, you might say, "I don't have all the answers, but I'm committed to finding a solution with your input."

4. **Maintain a Growth Mindset**

Authentic self-belief acknowledges that you're a work in progress. Embrace challenges as opportunities to grow, and be open to feedback.

- ◦ **Mantra:** "I am capable of learning, growing, and improving."

5. **Radiate Positivity**

A confident person exudes optimism and resilience. While it's important to acknowledge difficulties, focus on solutions rather than dwelling on problems.

- ◦ **Practice:** When discussing challenges, emphasize your plan to address them rather than the obstacles themselves.

6. **Align Your Presence with Your Confidence**

How you present yourself affects how others perceive your confidence.

- ◦ **Body Language:** Stand tall, maintain eye contact, and use open gestures.
- ◦ **Appearance:** Dress in a way that makes you feel comfortable and empowered. This isn't about impressing others—it's about feeling your best.

7. **Inspire Others with Your Confidence**

Radiating confidence isn't about overshadowing others; it's about uplifting them. Authentic self-belief encourages collaboration, empowerment, and mutual respect.

- ◦ **Action Step:** Celebrate others' successes and encourage their efforts, creating an environment where confidence is contagious.

The Balance Between Confidence and Humility

Owning your power doesn't mean becoming arrogant or overconfident. Confidence and humility are not opposites—they complement each other.

1. **Recognize Your Limits**

   Confidence acknowledges strengths, while humility recognizes areas for growth. Be honest about what you know and open to learning.

2. **Seek Input and Collaboration**

   A confident person values the perspectives of others and welcomes constructive feedback.

   ○ **Action Step:** Ask for input on your work or ideas, and approach feedback with curiosity rather than defensiveness.

3. **Celebrate Others' Achievements**

   Authentic confidence isn't threatened by others' success. Instead, it celebrates and learns from it.

   ○ **Tip:** Avoid comparison by focusing on your unique journey and strengths.

Your Confidence Power in Action

Owning your power means embracing your imperfections, learning from setbacks, and radiating authenticity in everything you do. Confidence is not a mask you wear; it's an expression of your true self.

Here's how to put this into action:

1. **Daily Affirmations:** Begin each day with a positive statement about your abilities and worth.
2. **Reflect on Challenges:** At the end of each week, review any setbacks you faced and the lessons you learned from them.
3. **Act with Integrity:** Align your choices with your values, even when it's difficult.
4. **Celebrate Progress:** Recognize and reward your achievements, no matter how small.

By maintaining confidence during setbacks and radiating authentic self-belief, you'll not only transform your own life but also inspire those around you. In the next chapter, we'll explore how to sustain your confidence over the long term, ensuring that it becomes a lasting and empowering force in your life.

Appendix A: Exercises for Daily Confidence Boosts

Confidence, like any skill, improves with consistent practice. Integrating daily exercises into your routine can help you cultivate and maintain a strong sense of self-belief. This appendix provides a collection of practical, actionable exercises designed to give your confidence a boost every day. These activities focus on self-awareness, positive reinforcement, and actionable steps toward personal growth.

Morning Confidence Exercises

Start your day with a foundation of positivity and self-assurance by practicing these morning routines:

1. Daily Affirmations

Affirmations are powerful tools for reprogramming your mindset and building confidence.

- **How to Practice:**
    - Stand in front of a mirror and repeat 3–5 affirmations aloud. Examples include:
        - "I am capable of achieving my goals."
        - "I deserve success and happiness."
        - "I am confident, resilient, and strong."
    - Speak with conviction and maintain eye contact with your reflection.
- **Tip:** Write down your affirmations on sticky notes and place them where you'll see them often, such as on your mirror or desk.

2. Visualize Success

Visualization helps you mentally rehearse confidence-boosting scenarios.

- **How to Practice:**
    - Close your eyes and take a few deep breaths.
    - Imagine yourself succeeding in an upcoming challenge or goal. Picture every detail: your actions, your emotions, and the positive outcome.
    - Focus on the sense of accomplishment and confidence you feel in that moment.

3. Gratitude Practice

Gratitude shifts your focus from what's lacking to what's abundant in your life, creating a positive mindset.

- **How to Practice:**
    - Write down three things you're grateful for each morning.
    - Reflect on how these things contribute to your well-being and success.
    - End your gratitude list with a statement of self-appreciation, such as, "I am grateful for my ability to learn and grow."

Midday Confidence Boosters

Keep your confidence strong throughout the day with these quick exercises:

4. Power Posing

Adopting confident body language can immediately boost your self-assurance.

- **How to Practice:**
    - Stand in a "power pose" for two minutes, such as the Superman pose (hands on hips, chest out, and chin slightly raised) or the Victory pose (arms raised in a V-shape).
    - Focus on feeling empowered and assertive as you hold the pose.

5. Accomplishment Journaling

Reflecting on your achievements reinforces your belief in your abilities.

- **How to Practice:**
    - Take five minutes to jot down recent accomplishments, no matter how small.
        - Examples: "I completed my workout," "I contributed a great idea in a meeting," or "I reached out to a friend I hadn't spoken to in a while."
    - Review your list whenever self-doubt creeps in.

6. Challenge Your Inner Critic

Reframe negative self-talk into positive, constructive thoughts.

- **How to Practice:**
    - Write down a negative thought you've had about yourself.
    - Challenge it with evidence to the contrary. For example:
        - Negative Thought: "I'm terrible at public speaking."
        - Reframe: "I've successfully delivered presentations before, and I'm improving with practice."
    - Replace the negative thought with an empowering one, such as, "I'm learning and getting better every day."

Evening Confidence Wind-Downs

End your day on a high note by reflecting on your progress and setting a positive tone for tomorrow.

7. Confidence Reflection Journal

Reflecting on your day helps you acknowledge your wins and identify areas for growth.

- **How to Practice:**
    - Answer these questions in a journal before bed:
        - What did I do well today?
        - How did I show confidence in my actions?
        - What can I do tomorrow to build on today's progress?
    - Focus on celebrating small wins, such as speaking up in a meeting or trying something new.

8. Self-Compassion Exercise

End your day with kindness toward yourself.

- **How to Practice:**
    - Reflect on a moment during the day when you felt self-doubt or disappointment.
    - Write a compassionate response to yourself, as if you were comforting a friend. For example:
        - "It's okay that things didn't go perfectly today. You're learning and doing your best, and that's what matters."

9. Future Success Visualization

Plant the seeds of tomorrow's confidence by envisioning success.

- **How to Practice:**
  - Close your eyes and visualize how you want tomorrow to unfold.
  - Picture yourself acting with confidence, overcoming challenges, and ending the day proud of your achievements.

On-the-Spot Confidence Boosters

For moments when you need an immediate confidence boost, try these quick exercises:

10. The Five-Second Rule

When hesitation strikes, count down from five and take action.

- **How to Practice:**
  - As soon as you feel self-doubt creeping in, say to yourself, "5-4-3-2-1, go!"
  - Take a small, courageous step toward your goal, such as introducing yourself to someone new or starting a challenging task.

11. Anchoring Technique

Use a physical anchor to recall a moment of confidence.

- **How to Practice:**
  - Think of a time when you felt exceptionally confident and successful.
  - Pair that memory with a physical gesture, such as pressing your thumb and index finger together.
  - In moments of doubt, repeat the gesture to mentally "anchor" yourself to that positive experience.

12. Confidence-Boosting Playlist

Music can instantly uplift your mood and energy.

- **How to Practice:**
    - Create a playlist of songs that make you feel empowered and confident.
    - Listen to it before tackling a challenge or when you need a quick boost.

Weekly Confidence Ritual

Dedicate time each week to deepen your confidence with a focused ritual:

13. Strengths Inventory

Take stock of your skills, talents, and qualities.

- **How to Practice:**
    - Set aside 30 minutes to list your strengths and accomplishments.
    - Reflect on how you've used these strengths in the past and how they can help you achieve future goals.

14. Confidence Goals Review

Evaluate your progress toward confidence related goals.

- **How to Practice:**
    - Review your goals and assess what's working and what needs adjustment.
    - Set one specific goal for the coming week to stretch your confidence, such as speaking up in a meeting or trying a new activity.

Conclusion: Building a Confidence Habit

These exercises are not one-time activities—they are habits to incorporate into your daily and weekly routine. The more consistently you practice them, the more natural and ingrained your confidence will become. Whether you're starting your day with affirmations, reflecting on your wins, or using on-the-spot techniques, each exercise contributes to a stronger, more resilient sense of self-belief.

Confidence is built one step at a time, and these exercises ensure you're taking intentional steps every day. Let this appendix serve as your toolkit for cultivating lasting confidence and owning your power in every area of your life.

<u>Message from the Author:</u>

I hope you enjoyed this book, I love astrology and knew there was not a book such as this out on the shelf. I love metaphysical items as well. Please check out my other books:

-Life of Government Benefits

-My life of Hell

-My life with Hydrocephalus

-Red Sky

-World Domination:Woman's rule

-World Domination:Woman's Rule 2: The War

-Life and Banishment of Apophis: book 1

-The Kidney Friendly Diet

-The Ultimate Hemp Cookbook

-Creating a Dispensary(legally)

-Cleanliness throughout life: the importance of showering from childhood to adulthood.

-Strong Roots: The Risks of Overcoddling children

-Hemp Horoscopes: Cosmic Insights and Earthly Healing

- Celestial Hemp Navigating the Zodiac: Through the Green Cosmos

-Astrological Hemp: Aligning The Stars with Earth's Ancient Herb

-The Astrological Guide to Hemp: Stars, Signs, and Sacred Leaves

-Green Growth: Innovative Marketing Strategies for your Hemp Products and Dispensary

-Cosmic Cannabis

-Astrological Munchies

-Henry The Hemp

-Zodiacal Roots: The Astrological Soul Of Hemp

- **Green Constellations: Intersection of Hemp and Zodiac**

-Hemp in The Houses: An astrological Adventure Through The Cannabis Galaxy

-Galactic Ganja Guide

Heavenly Hemp

Zodiac Leaves

Doctor Who Astrology

Cannastrology

Stellar Satvias and Cosmic Indicas

Celestial Cannabis: A Zodiac Journey

AstroHerbology: The Sky and The Soil: Volume 1

AstroHerbology:Celestial Cannabis:Volume 2

Cosmic Cannabis Cultivation

The Starry Guide to Herbal Harmony: Volume 1

The Starry Guide to Herbal Harmony: Cannabis Universe: Volume 2

Yugioh Astrology: Astrological Guide to Deck, Duels and more

Nightmare Mansion: Echoes of The Abyss

Nightmare Mansion 2: Legacy of Shadows

Nightmare Mansion 3: Shadows of the Forgotten

Nightmare Mansion 4: Echoes of the Damned

The Life and Banishment of Apophis: Book 2

Nightmare Mansion: Halls of Despair

Healing with Herb: Cannabis and Hydrocephalus

Planetary Pot: Aligning with Astrological Herbs: Volume 1

Fast Track to Freedom: 30 Days to Financial Independence Using AI, Assets, and Agile Hustles

Cosmic Hemp Pathways

How to Become Financially Free in 30 Days: 10,000 Paths to Prosperity

Zodiacal Herbage: Astrological Insights: Volume 1

Nightmare Mansion: Whispers in the Walls

The Daleks Invade Atlantis
Henry the hemp and Hydrocephalus

10X The Kidney Friendly Diet
Cannabis Universe: Adult coloring book
Hemp Astrology: The Healing Power of the Stars
Zodiacal Herbage: Astrological Insights: Cannabis Universe: Volume 2
Planetary Pot: Aligning with Astrological Herbs: Cannabis Universes: Volume 2
Doctor Who Meets the Replicators and SG-1: The Ultimate Battle for Survival
Nightmare Mansion: Curse of the Blood Moon
The Celestial Stoner: A Guide to the Zodiac
Cosmic Pleasures: Sex Toy Astrology for Every Sign
Hydrocephalus Astrology: Navigating the Stars and Healing Waters
Lapis and the Mischievous Chocolate Bar

Celestial Positions: Sexual Astrology for Every Sign
Apophis's Shadow Work Journal: : A Journey of Self-Discovery and Healing
Kinky Cosmos: Sexual Kink Astrology for Every Sign
Digital Cosmos: The Astrological Digimon Compendium
Stellar Seeds: The Cosmic Guide to Growing with Astrology
Apophis's Daily Gratitude Journal

Cat Astrology: Feline Mysteries of the Cosmos
The Cosmic Kama Sutra: An Astrological Guide to Sexual Positions
Unleash Your Potential: A Guided Journal Powered by AI Insights
Whispers of the Enchanted Grove

Cosmic Pleasures: An Astrological Guide to Sexual Kinks

369, 12 Manifestation Journal

Whisper of the nocturne journal(blank journal for writing or drawing)

The Boogey Book

Locked In Reflection: A Chastity Journey Through Locktober

Generating Wealth Quickly:

How to Generate $100,000 in 24 Hours

Star Magic: Harness the Power of the Universe

The Flatulence Chronicles: A Fart Journal for Self-Discovery

The Doctor and The Death Moth

Seize the Day: A Personal Seizure Tracking Journal

The Ultimate Boogeyman Safari: A Journey into the Boogie World and Beyond

Whispers of Samhain: 1,000 Spells of Love, Luck, and Lunar Magic: Samhain Spell Book

Apophis's guides:

Witch's Spellbook Crafting Guide for Halloween

<u>Frost & Flame: The Enchanted Yule Grimoire of 1000 Winter Spells</u>

<u>The Ultimate Boogey Goo Guide & Spooky Activities for Halloween Fun</u>

Harmony of the Scales: A Libra's Spellcraft for Balance and Beauty

The Enchanted Advent: 36 Days of Christmas Wonders

Nightmare Mansion: The Labyrinth of Screams

Harvest of Enchantment: 1,000 Spells of Gratitude, Love, and Fortune for Thanksgiving

The Boogey Chronicles: A Journal of Nightly Encounters and Shadowy Secrets

The 12 Days of Financial Freedom: A Step-by-Step Christmas Countdown to Transform Your Finances

Sigil of the Eternal Spiral Blank Journal

A Christmas Feast: Timeless Recipes for Every Meal

Holiday Stress-Free Solutions: A Survival Guide to Thriving During the Festive Season

Yu-Gi-Oh! Holiday Gifting Mastery: The Ultimate Guide for Fans and Newcomers Alike

Holiday Harmony: A Hydrocephalus Survival Guide for the Festive Season

Celestial Craft: The Witch's Almanac for 2025 – A Cosmic Guide to Manifestations, Moons, and Mystical Events

Doctor Who: The Toymaker's Winter Wonderland

Tulsa King Unveiled: A Thrilling Guide to Stallone's Mafia Masterpiece

Pendulum Craft: A Complete Guide to Crafting and Using Personalized Divination Tools

Nightmare Mansion: Santa's Eternal Eve

Starlight Noel: A Cosmic Journey through Christmas Mysteries

The Dark Architect: Unlocking the Blueprint of Existence

Surviving the Embrace: The Ultimate Guide to Encounters with The Hugging Molly

The Enchanted Codex: Secrets of the Craft for Witches, Wiccans, and Pagans

Harvest of Gratitude: A Complete Thanksgiving Guide

Yuletide Essentials: A Complete Guide to an Authentic and Magical Christmas

Celestial Smokes: A Cosmic Guide to Cigars and Astrology

Living in Balance: A Comprehensive Survival Guide to Thriving with Diabetes Insipidus

Cosmic Symbiosis: The Venom Zodiac Chronicles

The Cursed Paw of Ambition

Cosmic Symbiosis: The Astrological Venom Journal

Celestial Wonders Unfold: A Stargazer's Guide to the Cosmos (2024-2029)

The Ultimate Black Friday Prepper's Guide: Mastering Shopping Strategies and Savings

Cosmic Sales: The Astrological Guide to Black Friday Shopping

Legends of the Corn Mother and Other Harvest Myths

Whispers of the Harvest: The Corn Mother's Journal

The Evergreen Spellbook

The Doctor Meets the Boogeyman

The White Witch of Rose Hall's SpellBook

The Gingerbread Golem's Shadow: A Study in Sweet Darkness

The Gingerbread Golem Codex: An Academic Exploration of Sweet Myths

The Gingerbread Golem Grimoire: Sweet Magicks and Spells for the Festive Witch

The Curse of the Gingerbread Golem

10-minute Christmas Crafts for kids

<u>Christmas Crisis Solutions: The Ultimate Last-Minute Survival Guide</u>

Gingerbread Golem Recipes: Holiday Treats with a Magical Twist

The Infinite Key: Unlocking Mystical Secrets of the Ages

Enchanted Yule: A Wiccan and Pagan Guide to a Magical and Memorable Season

Dinosaurs of Power: Unlocking Ancient Magick

Astro-Dinos: The Cosmic Guide to Prehistoric Wisdom

Gallifrey's Yule Logs: A Festive Doctor Who Cookbook

The Dino Grimoire: Secrets of Prehistoric Magick

The Gift They Never Knew They Needed

The Gingerbread Golem's Culinary Alchemy: Enchanting Recipes for a Sweetly Dark Feast

A Time Lord Christmas: Holiday Adventures with the Doctor

Krampusproofing Your Home: Defensive Strategies for Yule

Silent Frights: A Collection of Christmas Creepypastas to Chill Your Bones

Santa Raptor's Jolly Carnage: A Dino-Claus Christmas Tale

Prehistoric Palettes: A Dino Wicca Coloring Journey

The Christmas Wishkeeper Chronicles

The Starlight Sleigh: A Holiday Journey

Elf Secrets: The True Magic of the North Pole

Candy Cane Conjurations

Cooking with Kids: Recipes Under 20 Minutes

Doctor Who: The TARDIS Confiscation

The Anxiety First Aid Kit: Quick Tools to Calm Your Mind

Frosty Whispers: A Winter's Tale

The Infinite Key: Unlocking the Secrets to Prosperity, Resilience, and Purpose

The Grasping Void: Why You'll Regret This Purchase

Astrology for Busy Bees: Star Signs Simplified

The Instant Focus Formula: Cut Through the Noise

The Secret Language of Colors: Unlocking the Emotional Codes

Sacred Fossil Chronicles: Blank Journal

The Christmas Cottage Miracle

Feeding Frenzy: Graboid-Inspired Recipes

Manifest in Minutes: The Quick Law of Attraction Guide

The Symbiote Chronicles: Doctor Who's Venomous Journey

Think Tiny, Grow Big: The Minimalist Mindset

The Energy Key: Unlocking Limitless Motivation

New Year, New Magic: Manifesting Your Best Year Yet

Unstoppable You: Mastering Confidence in Minutes

Infinite Energy: The Secret to Never Feeling Drained

Lightning Focus: Mastering the Art of Productivity in a Distracted World

Saturnalia Manifestation Magick: A Guide to Unlocking Abundance During the Solstice

Graboids and Garland: The Ultimate Tremors-Themed Christmas Guide

12 Nights of Holiday Magic

The Power of Pause: 60-Second Mindfulness Practices

The Quick Reset: How to Reclaim Your Life After Burnout

The Shadow Eater: A Tale of Despair and Survival

The Micro-Mastery Method: Transform Your Skills in Just Minutes a Day

Reclaiming Time: How to Live More by Doing Less

Chronovore: The Eternal Nexus

The Mind Reset: Unlocking Your Inner Peace in a Chaotic World

If you want solar for your home go here: https://www.harborsolar.live/apophisenterprises/

Get Some Tarot cards: https://www.makeplayingcards.com/sell/ apophis-occult-shop

Get some shirts: https://www.bonfire.com/store/apophis-shirt-emporium/

<u>Instagrams:</u>
@apophis_enterprises,
@apophisbookemporium,
@apophisscardshop
Twitter: @apophisenterpr1
 Tiktok:@apophisenterprise
Youtube: @sg1fan23477, @FiresideRetreatKingdom
Hive: @sg1fan23477
CheeLee: @SG1fan23477

Podcast: Apophis Chat Zone: https://open.spotify.com/show/ 5zXbrCLEV2xzCp8ybrfHsk?si=fb4d4fdbdce44dec

Newsletter: https://apophiss-newsletter-27c897.beehiiv.com/

If you want to support me or see posts of other projects that I have come over to: **buymeacoffee.com/mpetchinskg**

I post there daily several times a day

Get your Dinowicca or Christmas themed digital products, especially Santa Raptor songs and other musics. Here: **https://sg1fan23477.gumroad.com**

Apophis Yuletide Digital has not only digital Christmas items, but it will have all things with Dinowicca as well as other Digital products.

www.ingramcontent.com/pod-product-compliance
Lightning Source LLC
Chambersburg PA
CBHW061312140726
47998CB00006B/2361